WHAT A MAP CAN DO

To Nora, who always maps a beautiful path.

—GB

To my aunt Rita. I love you, *zia*!

—AL

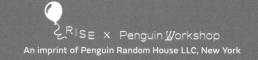
RISE x Penguin Workshop
An imprint of Penguin Random House LLC, New York

First published in the United States of America by Rise × Penguin Workshop, an imprint of Penguin Random House LLC, New York, 2023

Text copyright © 2023 by Gabrielle Balkan
Illustrations copyright © 2023 by Alberto Lot

Visit us online at penguinrandomhouse.com.

Library of Congress Cataloging-in-Publication Data is available.

Manufactured in China

ISBN 9780593519981   10 9 8 7 6 5 4 3 2 1 HH

The text is set in FS Emeric.
The art was sketched with a pencil and created with Photoshop.

Edited by Cecily Kaiser
Designed by Maria Elias

WHAT A MAP CAN DO

WORDS BY
GABRIELLE
BALKAN

ART BY
ALBERTO
LOT

RISE
NEW YORK

Psst. Come a little closer.
I've got something to show you.

It's not a book and it's not a basketball.
It's not a portrait of my great-grand-raccoon.

It's something small, like me.
And it shows you something big.

Look: It's a **map**.

A map can show us a bird's-eye view of a place.
It lets you see a place from above . . .
and you don't even have to be a bird.

My room has lots of cool things in it. The map of
my room shows where the important things are,
from above.

I draw at my desk.
Can you find it on
the map?

I snuggle in my bed.
Can you find it on
the map?

Can you find my
stuffed animal?
It's on my bed.
Point to it!

7

A MAP OF MY HOUSE

You are so good at finding things.
I need you as my map partner!

A map shows us where things are.

This map shows us that the blue couch is in the living room.

It shows us that the gray toilet is in the bathroom.

Where on the map is the stove?
Oooh, it looks hot!

The last thing we need to find is my scooter. It's in the hallway.

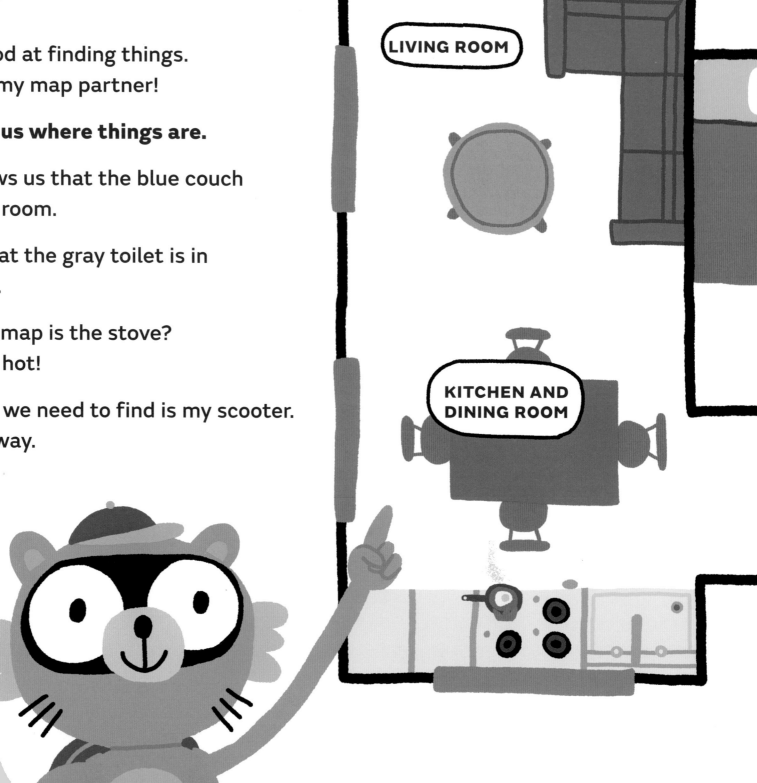

LIVING ROOM

KITCHEN AND DINING ROOM

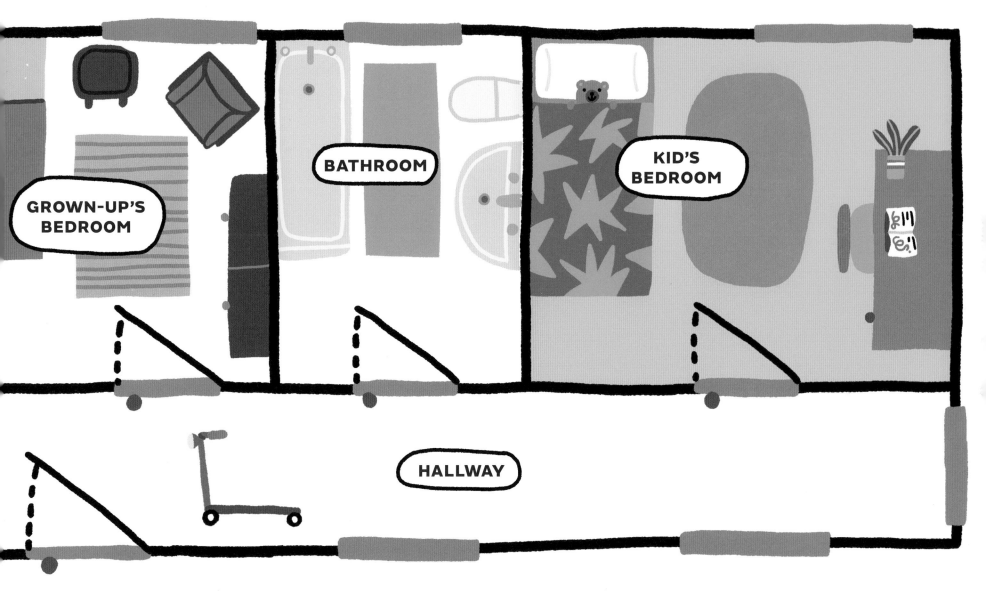

GROWN-UP'S BEDROOM

BATHROOM

KID'S BEDROOM

HALLWAY

A MAP OF MY NEIGHBORHOOD

A map is a tool that can help us get to where we want to go.

If we want to play outside, we can scoot to the neighborhood playground.

Can you find the path from my home to the playground? (This symbol shows you where I am on the map.)

How many houses will we pass on our way?

HERE'S MY HOUSE!

HERE'S THE PLAYGROUND!

We made it! Thank you, map!

Now that we're here, we can swing and slide and climb and hop!

What should we do first?

That was fun. Where to next?
Let's look at another map!

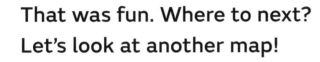

CITY MAP

My small neighborhood is in a big city. There's so much to explore!

A map uses symbols to show us all the places we can go.

The map's **key** tells us what the symbols mean.

We could walk to the library. Do you see the symbol for the library?

We could scoot to the hardware store. Can you find the symbol for the hardware store?

We could even ride a bus. Yes, let's do that! Now, where's the bus stop?

HERE'S MY HOUSE!

KEY

BUS STOP

HARDWARE STORE

LIBRARY

MARKET

MUSEUM

MY STARTING PLACE

Congratulations! You found the bus stop. And I found a bus *map* to show us where the buses go.

The white circles show where we can get on and off the bus. Those are bus stops.

Find a bus stop on the orange line. Where could we go on the pink line? Let's take the green line to the museum.

How many bus stops will it take us to get to the museum?

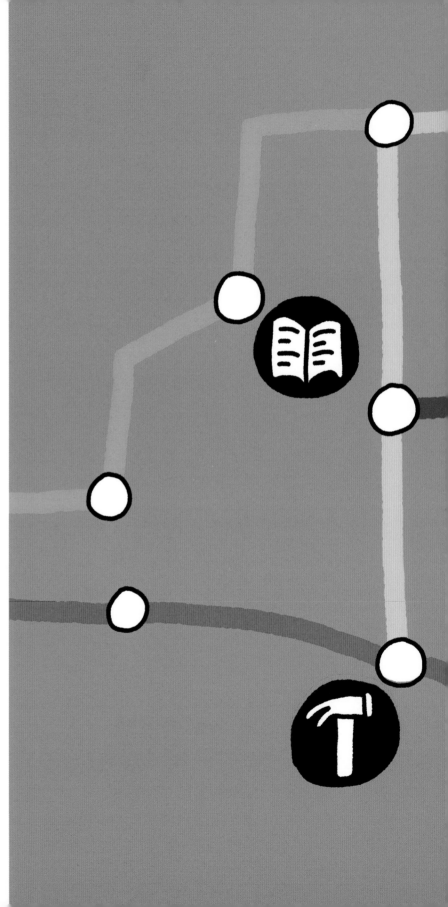

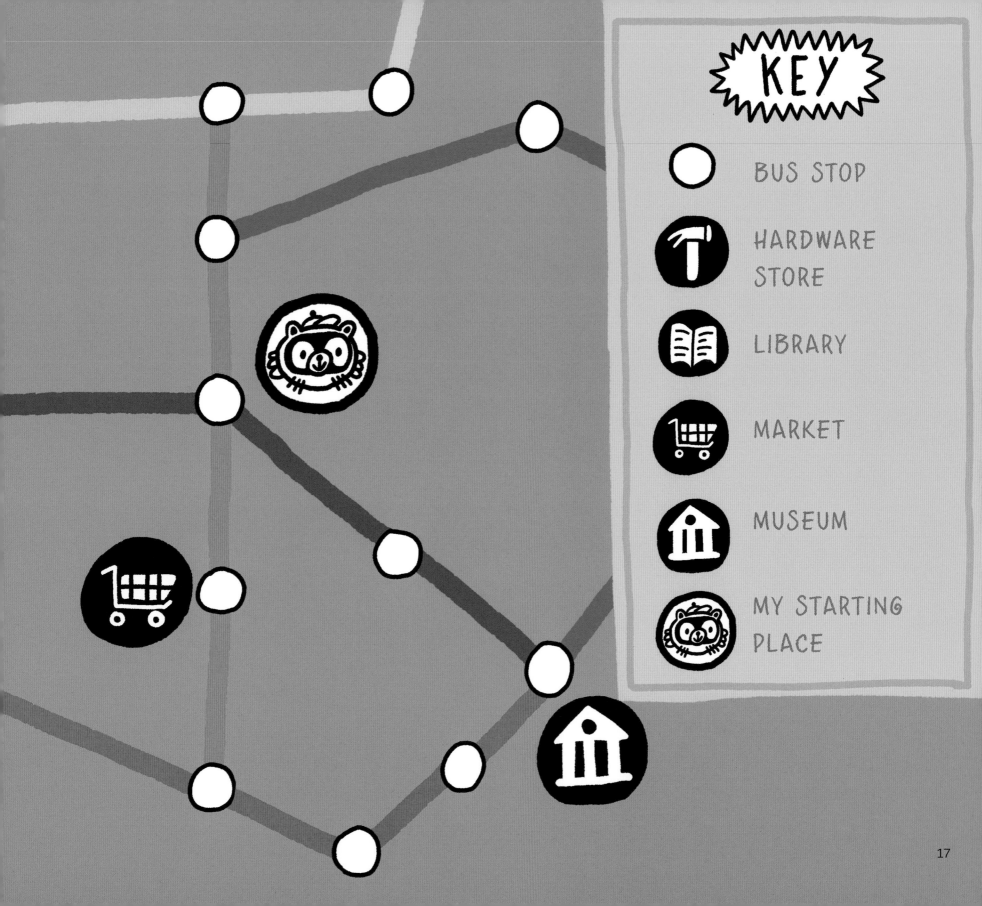

Success! We're here!

A map of the museum helps us plan our visit.

I want to explore the Special Exhibit and the café.
We can get animal crackers in the café.
Can you help me find my path?

KEY

A MAP OF THE INSIDE OF MY BODY

A map can show us things we cannot see,
funny things, and even both at once!
This funny map shows the path that
the animal crackers will take to get
from my mouth to my stomach. Yum!
What else can you see in my body map?
What would be in a map of your body?

That snack gave me just the right
amount of energy to take us on our
next adventure.

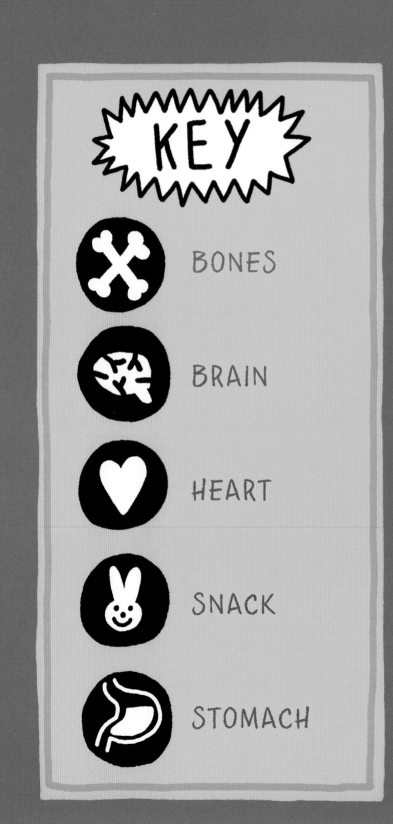

KEY

BONES

BRAIN

HEART

SNACK

STOMACH

Museum maps help you find
your way around a museum.

City maps help you find
your way around a city.

But what if you want to find
your way to *another* city?

ROAD MAP

A road map can help us travel from one city to the next, one state to the next, and even one country to the next!

Some roads are slow. Some roads are fast! Some roads have names. Some roads have numbers. Every road has road signs.

Which road should we take to get to the National Forest? We can take different roads next time.

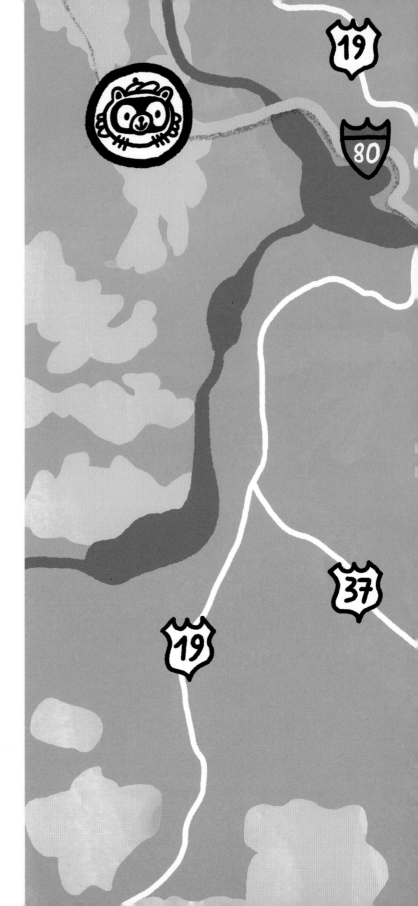

NATIONAL FOREST MAP

You have excellent navigation skills! You brought us to the National Forest.

A map shows you which direction to go. On this map, a **compass rose** helps with that!

A compass rose is a picture that shows you how to find north and other directions on your map.

We go **north** to find the Welcome Center.

We hike **east** to find the campgrounds.

We skip **south** to find the showers.

We drive **west** to get back to my city.

Let's visit the Welcome Center to pick up a trail map! The compass rose will tell you the direction we need to go.

KEY

CAMPGROUNDS

FIRST AID

INTERSTATE

PLAYGROUND

SHOWERS

WELCOME CENTER

MY STARTING PLACE

NORTH

WEST

EAST

SOUTH

27

TRAIL MAP

Nice work! Now we've got our trail map. **A map can show us what to expect.**

There is more than one hiking trail in this forest. Some are easier and some are harder. Some are longer and some are shorter. Each trail has its own color.

Which trail should we take to get from the Welcome Center to the campgrounds? A long or a short trail? You choose!

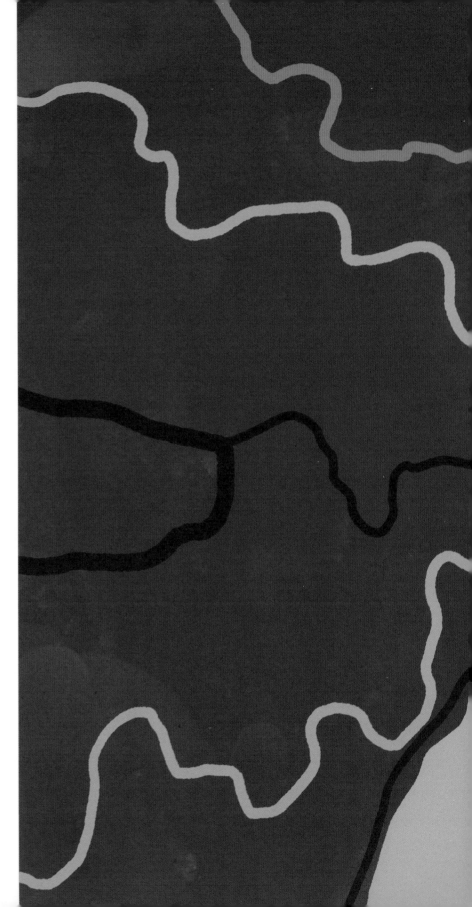

KEY

BIKE TRAIL

EASY TRAIL

MEDIUM TRAIL

HARD TRAIL

CAMPGROUNDS

WELCOME
CENTER

MY STARTING
PLACE

NORTH

WEST

EAST

SOUTH

29

That was a good choice. We got here in plenty of time to set up my tent. There is a spot for my bedtime book and a spot for my flashlight.

I wonder if I'll need my raincoat. What map can I check to help me answer that?

WEATHER MAP

A weather map shows us if it will rain or snow or hail or shine in our area. Then we know whether we need rain boots, snow boots, a helmet, or sunglasses! A weather map changes every day.

According to this map, I won't need my raincoat until tomorrow night. There are no clouds in the sky. We should be able to see the stars tonight!

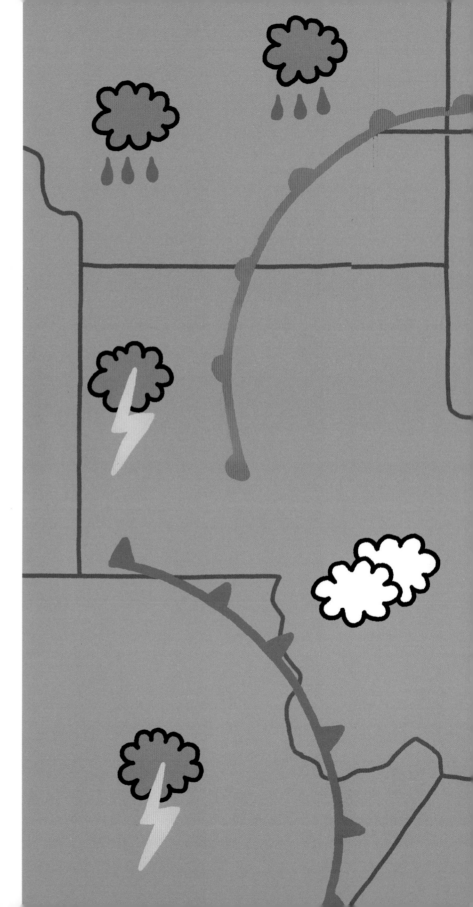

KEY

SUNNY

PARTLY SUNNY

CLOUDY

RAINY

THUNDERSTORM

WARM AIR

COLD AIR

MY STARTING PLACE

STAR MAP

Wow. The stars are beautiful.

A map can help us understand the sky, too.

This star map has lines drawn between certain stars to make patterns, shapes, and animals. These are called **constellations**.

Point to the constellations you see.

I see one that reminds me that it's almost time to go home.

KEY

STAR

CONSTELLATION

35

What a wild ride we had!

I love to use maps. Especially when they bring me someplace I love.

Where do you think we should go on our next adventure?

Let's use a map to get there!

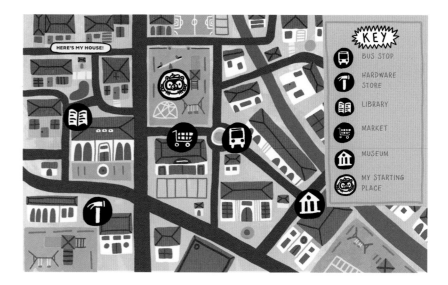

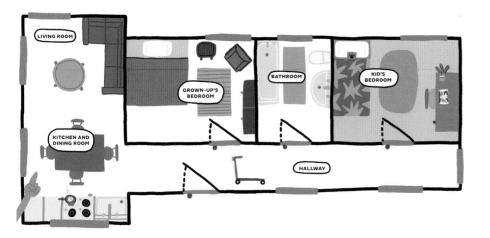

A MAP OF MY HOUSE

pages 8–9

A map shows us where things are.

A MAP OF MY NEIGHBORHOOD

pages 10–11

A map is a tool that can help us get to where we want to go.

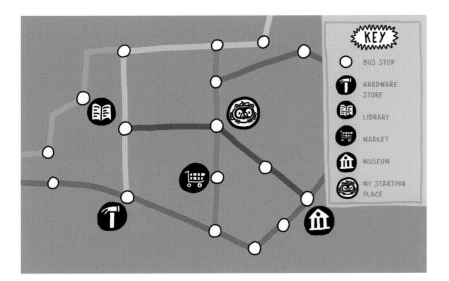

BUS MAP

pages 16–17

A map can show us which buses to take.

MUSEUM MAP

pages 18–19

A map can help us plan a visit to a museum.

A MAP OF THE INSIDE OF MY BODY

pages 20—21

A map can show us things we cannot see.

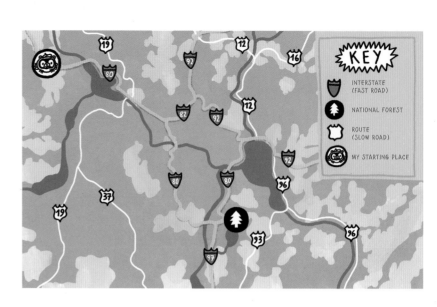

ROAD MAP

pages 24—25

A map can help us travel from one city to the next.

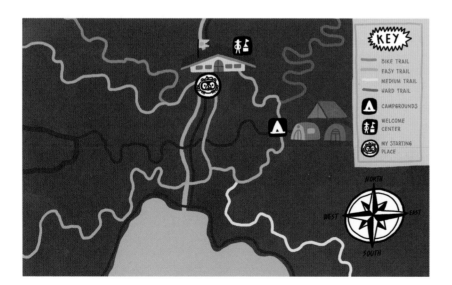

TRAIL MAP

pages 28—29

A map can show us what to expect.

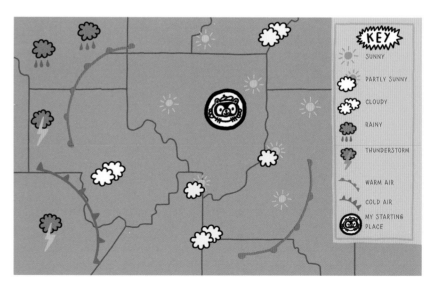

WEATHER MAP

pages 32—33

A map can help us be prepared.

NATIONAL FOREST MAP

pages 26—27

A map shows you which direction to go.

STAR MAP

pages 34—35

A map can help us understand a new place.